Surfaces Slipping Beneath

MARK NUTTALL

THE CHOIR PRESS

Copyright © 2026 Mark Nuttall

All rights reserved. No part of this publication may be reproduced or transmitted in any form or by any means, electronic or mechanical including photocopying, recording or any information storage or retrieval system, without prior permission in writing from the publishers.

The right of Mark Nuttall to be identified as the author of this work has been asserted by him in accordance with the Copyright, Designs and Patents Act 1988

First published in the United Kingdom in 2026 by The Choir Press

ISBN 978-1-78963-591-1

Cover image by Mark Nuttall

For Millie

Contents

Shale	1
The Mountain	2
Black Smoke	4
Chwarel	7
Pandy Heap	10
Reckoning	15
Maes-y-Groes	16
Gwyniad	18
Gwynt y Môr	20
The Slow Unmaking	23
Chicken Bones	25
Tide-Edge Hunter	28
Mortarless Joints	30
Glimmer	32
Windbreak	34
Shimmer	36
At the Water's Edge	37
Stone	39
Backen	40
Nizzly	42
Ackersprit	43
Fox Bench	44
Chester, 1744	45
Herringbone Road	47
Salt Blooms Rising	48
Rushbearing	50
Cat Grin	52
Crow Nets	53

Along the North and West Line	56
Larks	58
Marrowbone	60
Longhope	62
Shore Pebbles	64
Land Stones	66

Drift   67

Undertow	68
Fen Lanterns	70
Slipping Slack	72
Into the Long Remembering	73
Mud Crawler	76
Unremarked	77
Ferry	81
Within the Great Hill	82
Myrtle Corner	86
The Streets	89
Delicate Fracturing	91
The General Synopsis at 06.00	93
Denmark Strait	98
Far Ridge	101
Track Reappearing	103
Turnaround Point	105

Coda   107

Shale

The Mountain

We know this common ground as the Mountain,
although it does not rise sharply, on any side,
and is not especially lofty.

Its approaches are gradual,
rather than sudden,
its appearance subdued,
almost solemn.

Not everyone is curious enough
to turn from the high-speed road,
the expressway express-pressed between tidal flats
easing up to the pocked limestone approach.

Many are fixed on rushing
toward the higher hills, Eryri,
or the coast, the pier, penny arcades,

ferris wheel, pitch n' putt, caravan parks,
the sand, scraps and gull grabs.
Some just want to get home.

But here is weight, in the lead tips,
capped shafts, lime kilns, quarries,
and half-collapsed windlasses,

pressing down on a long history
that draws the land
into and around itself,

beneath the thin, crumpled skin
of grass and wildflowers,
into scooped-out earth.

I wander here, going along,
to find, uncover, discover
what lurks

sheltering
in rocky outcrops, damp hollows,
and cool shadowy corners.

Look closely, see the places
where the Mountain
bled out through the lacerations.

How astonishing, then,
to find the leaden land a refuge
for plants that survive
where others cannot.

A confidence to be flirtatious.
With knowing beauty.

Spring sandwort – the miners' white star –
thrives where ore was crushed, washed,
the waste swept away.

Heather, purple and pink, stitching
fraying from the bruised wounds,
spreads generously across the dry heath.

The Mountain draws breath
in a way that seems miraculous.

Black Smoke

Light dimmed and faded to rust
down there in the earth's dark maw
where they clawed, hacked, and stabbed.

Stabbed, stabbed at the copper heart
until it punctured and seeped
reddish orange in the candle glow.

Above it all, in the green blue,
and around the lakes, landscapes of extraction
in the sliced-away hillsides smudged with dust

were places to avoid, to ignore. Such unsightly
interruptions intruding into a quest
for the picturesque and solemn grandeur.

For those who looked for ancient ruins,
wandering in search of stone circles, harps,
cascades, horseshoe river turns and bardic relics,

the terraces shaped from song, prayer, and toil,
the yawning chasms, engine houses,
pit-wheels and spoil, offered no solace.

The hills and valleys were meant to hold myth,
romance, and ivy-clad castle walls, not foundries,
mounds of black rock or grimy smokestacks.

They could not escape the marks of industry,
nor refuse the offensive pungent greeting
of the tanneries and breweries.

The quarries, mines, the malodorous factories,
the roar and heat from the furnace blast,
the rag-clad children picking over slag,

the flea-ridden hovels in the romantic vale,
the puffs of black smoke were blemishes, nuisances,
spoiling the artist's view behind the abbey arches.

No matter if the effect was disturbed for those
who preferred to linger beside a pleasant waterfall,
enjoying a fine view of graceful hills topped with grey turrets,

some pedestrian travellers carried on and found
they had as much to say about the holes in the ground,
as they did about the sea meeting the land.

They described hidden underground rivers
draining into the estuary, curing the lame,
flat bottomed boats carrying coal and ore,

smouldering vats, lead turning to silver,
the wretched in the hideous cotton mills,
a ceaseless and horrid din on rugged heights,

grimy figures on the ridge, walking home
from the glitter lode in the dark chapels,
the weight of the hills dragging their legs down

to the gloomy town, the hammering still ringing,
living inside the wounds, pulling and scooping
the entrails from the dreary mountain

for the bubbling cauldron
feeling the abrasive ache at the gumline
kneeling at the holy spring

coughing themselves thin,
scarlet fever at the cot-side
sublimity in the horror.

Noise. Smoke. Ruin.
Bustle. Flame. Wonder.

Chwarel

I

The dawn breaks grey and cold,
boots crunch on fissile slate, oaths echo,
psalms, half-remembered,
are murmured on the descent.

Everything is running on a fractured bargain.
Walk on in with hymn books, go deep,
surfaces slipping beneath fingertips,
fragments scattered.

Flake, chasm, silence. Cleaved,
interleaved, between thin layers.
Slate knuckle scraping
along the chill underside.

Imprint staining, splintered shale
brittle under foot
knee crack, tongues licking
lips coated in mineral dust.

Drive the drill-rod,
lean and heave,
wield the hammer,
bring a fierce chisel and strong faith.

Cling to the creithiau
on the craggy face
deal with the coblynau
and heed the three knocks

the fickle mood,
haggle, breathe steady,
shoulder the powder keg,
step back, retreat

into tea steam,
tobacco and complaint,
thunder blast,
blue smoke.

Out again,
gritty bitter taste,
washed down,
squint through clouded eyes.

II

High poundage/low yield,
rybelwr looking for a stray slab,
rubblemen haul shards, slate-splitters, dressers
entice the beauty from the obdurate.

Quarrymen, bad-rock, rubbish.
Overseer. Quarry lord.
Equals? Never.
Not even when sliced down the middle.

There could be no sharper divide
between the butter-yellow stone
across the valley and the six days
of grind on the terraced galleries

on the shattered ledge,
down in the three throats,
the pallor of starvation on the faces
around the bread oven, along the bakehouse line

giving in, giving up to the slow erosion
of the place where a slight expression of joy
feels indulgent, as hope wears down against the scree,
the indifference of the land, and their Sunday best.

The village turns inward. The sermons cut deep.
The minister calls for restraint, pleads for patience.
Another thunders against injustice.
No traitor in the house.

Names repeat along the grave-path,
knitting chapel, church and school to twll,
ink and anger, muttering defiance,
chwarel quarrel, quarrying out the headstones.

Dissenters, radicals, try to let go
of grievances for the night
letting exhaustion quench and quell the anger.
Leave the living rock in peace for less insult.

Pandy Heap

The slag heap darkens at dusk,
slurping down the last dregs of light.
How can you call it a slag heap?
You may well ask.

It is a hill.
And it is growing greener.
An exemplar of reclamation.
A monument, some say.

A scar, some retort.
A hardened scab on the gash.
A spoil tip. A grubby mound.
A place of ghosts. Some shiver.

Let it stand.
Remove it.
Waste tip.
Wasted shale.

A miner's son says: ruin.
A man on the council says: heritage.
A woman next door says: rubbish.
A developer says: resource.

A relic, a burden.
Some are fond of it.
Others say bodies were bent,
snapped and broken for it.

A piece of history.
A mistake.
Unmake it.

How can the discarded
be thought of as something sacred?
How can such an eyesore,
be a thing of historical interest?

The black slope is the only hope
to honour the toil and the dead.
Not a track for bikes and quads.

But at least they're keeping themselves occupied,
not robbing and thieving, causing harm.

It's barren land. What's the fuss?
Why waste police time up on the waste.

The heap stays. Still,
but never settled. This hill.
A place where nothing flourishes
but argument.

Six million tonnes
of spent earth,
held in place
by decision
and indecision.

A woman at the bus stop recalls a time
when the air was thick with grime,
not all that long ago, not at all,

when the men retched and tried to cough up the dust
from below, sitting by their neat parlour firesides
burning the coal that was warming them and killing them.

Another, sixty-two, she says, wants the sky let back
in through her kitchen window.
She says she likes her hills to be made by God,
but does not complain about the noisy road and busy
　roundabout.

Just think.
Something good
can come from it,

all that slag,
taken away, reused
to reduce carbon emissions.

The world made anew
from the very stuff
that has harmed it.

Someone is still pushing the idea
of a museum, along with the winding gear
where local people can learn
about their community's mining legacy.

Go for picnics, walk the trails,
make an afternoon of it
in the country park,
take in the views and fresh air.

A good plan?
Where's the common sense in that!
All you need to do is ask those still alive
who lost their livelihoods,
when the last field closed,
who never found other work.

In the village pubs,
supping their mild, tasting bitter,
drowning their pride,
the barrel-chested old men
feel that history scratched
into the ripped lining of their black lungs.

Even more so when
they stand outside
in the rain for a smoke.

They remember making the tunnels,
picking away in the lamplight
against ancient seams with the water pooling,
the hollowing reaching upward to stain the air.

They recall the way they felt,
held their breath, thought of death,
when the ground heaved above them.
How they made the earth give.

They speak fondly of the horses leading them right
if they ever lost their light.
Coming over for titbits and bread,
going along steady, steady along.

Some remember stories handed down
of when the coal was worked with gunpowder,
when firedamp was given off freely,
the explosions, the charred bodies laid by the roadside.

The coal was not temperamental.
Political, yes of course, but did not insist
in its relinquishing that it only understood Welsh.
Like the slate did.

Leave it. That way the past,
never easy to talk about,
will never be removed from view.

Reckoning

Careful. The edge will let you go.
The drop is not too far out of reach.
The stones will loosen, tumble, and scatter.
You will hear the cliff crumble.

In this moment of reckoning,
when you feel the wind stiffen
and push at your shoulder blades,
find your firm foothold.

Grind the stones to dust if you must,
run the grains through your fingers,
confront the shattered truth,
gather up what stays.

Turn away from the churning,
the hail stones pelting, slashing sideways,
the raging, and the fury. Step back
from the steep fall to the battered shore.

Follow the steps of the nameless,
the forgotten, those who stood here before.
Ask about the old secrets, the longing.
Ask about all that is lamented.

Maes-y-Groes

I walk to the field of crossing,
the cross field,

the one we were brought up
to know as tethered tightly

to an old tale of a way over
the swallowing river,

of the ones who lie beneath, buried there,
and those who remained in their hiding places,

and another, the one I listened to most,
about the tall stone, a grey erratic,

standing, uprooting, shuffling, walking,
straying, touched, embraced

by the wanderers, the peregrinators,
seeking benediction, desiring blessings,

ragged and fading, praying for mercy,
living on bread and wind, solitude and visions,

picking their way through thirst and thistle,
between invocation and scripture, reverie and light,

abandoned to weather and ghostly saints
avoiding the trembling hare and the baying hounds

bone-pale with ears dipped in blood on the wild hunt
for the souls of those about to depart,

the fevered mouths and the listless,
those who beg for miracles and release,

seeking sanctuary near the blessed river shrine,
lingering by the waters of the curative well,

sheltering from the wind and rain
needing to feel the warm comforting breath

of something half beyond the known world,
or to find a way through the dark.

Gwyniad

Stranded fish.
A relic of the ice time,
a pale lingering memory
lurking in the waters of the lake
cradling old grief, giving shelter

conjured by a giant's sigh,
filled in from sorrow and melt,
vengeance, prophecy
and fierce enchantment
within the green sloped valley.

Shape of a salmon
taste of a trout,
mirror-bearer
slender, aloof,
of ethereal proportion.

Curious with its gentle fin, angled pupil,
coveted for its flesh, tasted,
yet seldom glimpsed, rarely biting,
careful of the spiny backed ruffe
settling in the spawning beds.

White as the cloud swirl in a winter sky,
moving closer to the shallow bays, muscling in
on the gravel beds of the glutinous snail,
almost argent in early light, glistening
with the sheen of frosted silver.

Shimmering, rippling,
beneath the surface,
a flickering invitation
to the watchers by the rocks,
an apparition

then vanishing swiftly,
sliding away,
scarcely troubling the wave
eluding hook, net and reason,
evading mortal snares,

yet succumbing to eutrophication,
leaching from the farmland,
slipping into the tight spaces
carved out by the pause
between legend and memory.

Gwynt y Môr

The land rolls gently,
drifts toward restless tides,
brambles thick as thieves,
sly chancers snatching

scratching skin, tearing away
the thin membrane,
sheep graze, browsing, nibbling
in the hedgerow shadows.

Muddy flats shimmer.
Look out far, to the stirring,
past sandbanks shifting slow,
across the salinity front

stretching wide.
The wind scuds
over the scumbled sea,
before turning, reeling,

bracing, becoming brisker,
sharpish, brushing,
woozy, groggy.
The fog rolls in.

Gwynt heli, gwynt o'r môr,
salt-laden sea wind. Planted deep,
gravel anchored, hammered
into the glacial till, future-facing

over the staggered chop
commanding the skyline. Spectral
some days, monumental others,
graceful, intrusive

in the geomorphic tumble
never still, never settled.
Rising above the lost,
ghosting over wrecks,

scattered cargoes,
fisher bones seasoned
and simmering low
in the megaripples.

Drone and hum,
a tidal prism mobilised
discernible pulses
transient motions,

resonant, residual
currents shifting,
barnacles, mussels
clinging to the welds,

ebb generation uplifting
amplitude reducing, deep
scour sediment drifting,
across intertidal zones.

Turning slowly,
drawing energy
from what
cannot be seen,

taking from what
cannot be held,
embodying hope and unease,
never closing the loop.

The Slow Unmaking

Coming down from the hill,
the one that is bare and paunch-shaped,
brooding alone in the great high ground,
west from the ridge of the white stone,
it begins to rain.

I stand still for a while and reflect
on how the water trickles
into the fissures on its back,
how it pools, freezes at night, and expands,
until what was once solid surrenders

to the steady persistence
of the slow choreography,
unhurried, splitting,
wearing the rock smooth,
exposing the layers with a slow unmaking.

I too am weathering.
Wearing away.
Not diminished.
Not yet, but a little more eroded,
more rounded,

no longer unmarred,
a little more brittle,
a little less sharp,
bending under a pressing weight,
silvered and splintered, slightly scarred,

losing layers, gaining lines,
shedding certainties,
gradually hollowed,
but not empty, creased,
skin quietly marked,

bearing inscriptions on flesh,
harsh in defiance,
yet accepting the weakening,
the gentle reclaiming,
the subtle sculpting,

the gradual reshaping,
conceding, embracing
the stripping away.
Until what remains is down to the grain.
Until whatever is left will be enough.

Chicken Bones

We should all make time for fieldwork,
to go exploring in the edgelands,

set off on an origin quest, investigating, probing
in the places from which the new fossils are appearing.

Go scrambling and scurrying away in landfill,
spend days crawling over the swelling dune lands

where chicken bones
interweave and fuse

with bottle caps,
ceramics, circuits,

and twisted cables
in the rank morass.

Pack trowels and spades
go digging down deep

through the layers
of forgotten excess,

go about getting grimy,
doing an archaeology

of the short-lived,
the hurried,

thirsty,
consuming,

the discarded
in metal oxide soils,

pulling batteries and rare earth shards from the putrid ooze,
wiping the slime from the cracked screens,

cutting the bandages away carefully from the embalmed
   emojis,
deciphering the pixel hieroglyphs with scholarly rigour

forming a picture of the swift, the restless,
the hastily indulgent, those too certain, those indifferent.

Uncovering traces and fingerprints,
dribbles of snapshot whittering chitter

unearthing the treasured artefacts of the selfie world,
transcribing the influencer narratives, shedding light on

the likes
the curated joy

the polished lives
the scrollers

the flawless feeds
the captions

the updates
the plugged ins

the followers
and borrowers

recording the weight of the instant grammes, the ounces,
the pounds, illuminating knowledge of the new dark ages,

resurrecting the remnants of everyday rituals, liturgies
and reckless waste trapped in midden amber.

Sifting through the curious debris,
the viral slogans,
questing for the origins of this epoch
that is all too brief to name,
yet long enough for shame,

defined by the silicon and rusted wire,
the endless murmuring,
the chatter compressed down,
abandoned, sedimented in the storied earth,
scratched and etched into the strata.

Tide-Edge Hunter

Do not walk with your back
to the sea. Not yet.
This beach has smooth black stones.
Do not pick up any, do not pocket them.

You say they look like the eyes
of grey seals keeping watch
on the gathering clouds.
Instead, you bend to pick up a dog whelk shell.

You find it while lifting
the olive brown fronds of egg wrack,
looking like tangled rosary beads,
holding fast on the rocky foreshore,

exposed at low tide, to see
what may be hiding beneath
from the harsh sun, sheltering
from the sandpaper raw wind.

Your attention was drawn first
to a flash of colour.
Silky tufts of red algae,
dense pom-pom clusters

clinging to the swollen nodes,
forming an intertidal bonsai garden.
You resist the urge to pop the wrack bladders
and rest the shell in your left palm.

It is cream-coloured.
You wonder aloud
if there are rare brown ones around.
It is slightly scoured.

The opening has been pulled apart,
suggesting the snail was devoured
where it lay inside.
Perhaps by a starfish pushing

its stomach out of its body
through the thick outer lip.
You admire the spiral sculpturing.
You run your finger along the teeth of its aperture,

and wonder about the speckled mussel hunter
that once lived within,
the slow, decisive, tongue barbed
patient driller.

Fierce predator. Weak prey.
You lay the dog whelk shell
at the tidemark.
You step back. Wait.

For the moment when the water
twists around and beyond its form,
allowing you to turn
and walk out into the eelgrass meadow.

Mortarless Joints

It begins in cracks
along the boundary wall,

soft spores settling
in damp crevices, catching

in clefts, seeping
through mortarless joints,

infiltrating, whorls,
light held in dew drops,

quilting sun-scored grey stone,
cushion mossing over the grooves

of fading initials carved
in an effort of being there,

where the top of the wall
is chalk-smeared, lichen freckled,

crustose, frost-pale,
persistent, dry, crumbling,

forming almost perfect circles
that can be rubbed to powder.

And there—
a slow unfurling from shadow

of furred fronds of fern,
root fine, green veined,

running in slender ribbons
along the loose slabs,

and English ivy—
three and five leaved—

spreading outward,
groping its way over,

filling the spaces
between grain and air,

binding soil and ruin,
growth and decay.

Glimmer

We do not meet the wild by chance, I thought,
threading my way towards the white crest,
walking across the lower side of the valley,
taking care to avoid the plants that are rare, and slight,
mindful of star sedge and bog-cotton skirts.

The light—soft, insistent—was a glimmer
spilling down Cadair Berwyn towards the tumulus,
the ancient funeral mounds and ring ditches
along the heathered ridges, over stone and tuft,
before brushing the plateau of Moel Sych.

I reached the old drovers' road where the moor opens,
keeping my eye on the giant's seat and the dry hill.
The summits were once located elsewhere on the map
when the lenses and trig points measured the wrong angles,
when the world was bent out of shape by visual tricks.

It seemed almost otherworldly that day in late summer,
walking there in the bleak, unmeasured and forlorn,
with the evening sun shearing across the spalled shale,
stretching slowly towards the edge of things,
its narrow arc brushing the cold rim of the earth.

The unknown does not reveal itself at once.
There is no clear line of sight leading to the uncanny.
It is not something you enter, move within,
and claim to know as if presence alone
were enough for understanding.

It hesitates, appears, pauses, unravels, loosens,
discloses intricate details, colours, cool textures,
flickerings. Like the soft susurrus of bilberry leaves,
and the grey-cloaked, soft-footed watchers,
those uncertain ones, the crag clingers,

crawling from the ribs of the longhouse
on the wind-scoured lip, half hiding,
slipping between the mist and drizzle,
trembling in the dusk, moving downhill,
drawn to the fire glow through the widening crack.

Windbreak

The gate at the end of the garden
is falling off its post and requires
a little effort to open and keep in place.

It leads onto a public footpath
that takes me across tilted, wavering fields
of scorched grass and baked mud.

The colour has drained from the land,
a field of rapeseed, uncut, has sunburned to husk,
the stalks brittle and wasted.

For the first stretch the path follows a brook,
more a crease through which rusty water wriggles along,
pooling briefly where it can in deeper runs.

Reaching a fence of sagging wire,
I follow along from post to post.
No-one else is walking here.

I arrive at a stile wearing into disuse.
Two stones and a splintered plank.
Brambles have taken the path and snag my ankles.

I make a short jump, relieved it is effortless,
across a shallow runnel, half-clogged
with the things that gather.

Near where a small group of cattle clusters
by a trough, another lone Hereford ambling up,
there is a windbreak. I head for it.

It stands along the spine.
Poplar and pine,
some larch,

leaning slightly.
Deliberate. Planted
between field and hill.

It was never intended to be beautiful, only useful.
There is no wind. The air clings to the thick stillness.
The world closes around me when I step into it.

Feeling cooler and slightly refreshed, but only just,
    I make my way
to the church with the embattled tower and its four
    gargoyles,
and consider the remains of the preaching cross.

Shimmer

Look at how the light on water dances,
how it splinters and crackles into sparks,
each presenting us with a fugacious glint
skimming across the surface of the lake.

The shimmer moves with the breeze
rippling out in pewter threads,
stretching toward the far shore,
quivering, beckoning, suggestive.

A fleeting moment that arrives,
catches the eye, cannot be grasped
or held tightly, and is gone as soon
as it decided to occur.

At the Water's Edge

What is it that seems to be gathering
at the water's edge?
It retreats, breaks apart,
returns, regroups, crawls back on shore.

As I watch, my chest tightens,
my body shudders.
To breathe steadily is an effort,
taking in air through whatever cracks I can.

Stone

Backen

They walk beside me
those forgotten mithered souls
throwing their fading shadows
on the fogh at the skrike of day.

These wraiths are fair perished
in the cowd slobber, shortwaisted
and bonesore in their festerment,
stumbling along in the worn grooves,

sloods and whabbles, bawtert wi' slutch
exposing roots and sandstone
over where the path folds up
on the cop, cutting through the field

down to the new fences lining the spaces
where the quillets used to be, dividing
the old ground from the frem folk
in the crescents that are waxing all around.

They go on, complaining, grumbling,
that the blusterous fou' weather
backens the ploughing
and makes for flaskerry work.

A scrawmy flaw runs, snell
along the adland's edge, nipping
at the muck-fork hands,
gawm-scarred from happing,

burning the knuckles,
seeking shelter, crowding,
chuntering in the shippen half-dark,
slow and thick, mending the day's plan

called back to the furrow
across the barren flat, stirring
over in the clottered ground
to strike a grudging yield.

I wonder who still hears their muttering
in the vanishing as the words
get trodden down in the mullock
and the chow and chump.

Nizzly

The lump of rock salt hangs
by a twine from its hook
set deep in the kitchen beam,

ungiving, yet dreeping slow
on the flagstone floor,
where the twitch clogs scutter,

sensing the mulsh,
the glow'ring clouds,
those mares' tails we see now,

the weather breeders, portending
the beginning of a nizzly morning,
a mumbling of ratching rain,

the pash that will likely flatten
the trellises in the garth.
The likelihood of a coarse day.

Ackersprit

The fields were the same colour as the cart tracks,
that summer when the rain did not arrive.

Some said the rituals had slipped from memory,
the correct way of doing things was long forgotten,
even though the Rogationtide procession had passed along

    on Ascension Day
        to beat the parish bounds
           and bless the earth.

There was nothing for the pikel to get hold of.
The grass wore thin, patched in the droughted pasture.

Not a green blade remained on the meadow,
the hay crop was light and short.
The grazing was gone, the cattle learned

    the patience of thirst,
        sheep drank in places
           where they never drank.

The air turned gritty, thick with dust and chaff.
The aldermen and the clergy led days of humiliation and
  prayer.

The land burnt up, the soil cracked open, yawning wide,
exposing the shoots that had mistaken their timing,
sprouting too soon, too feebly

    at both ends.
        The old life withered,
           the new life was unready.

Fox Bench

This is one clever way the earth tries to refuse:
an ancient trick, a subterranean smirk,
mocking, an illusion of permanence,
cunning as its namesake, deceptive,
tawny red even in the dim light.

A sham rock. Shallow hardened,
mischievous layer found where the land is foxy,
menacing, stubborn with water's grip.
Firm, tenacious, rust-threaded sandy loam,
obstinate, unmappable impediment underfoot.

A known underground horizon even to the clergymen
who wrote about the flint arrowheads
uncovered from the coarse sand and grit,
holding water, keeping the fields wet,
needing piercing to improve the land.

A shilling a rood for trenching and marling.
The turf men were diligent yet wary
not to overflow the excavations, taking care
not to let the bog up, turning soil to sludge,
otherwise, the land would keep its grudge.

Impervious, sly, defiant against the seep,
unbroken by the pressure of the rain,
resisting the penetration of the root,
defying a shattering by the plough
until it crumbles when the air reaches it.

Chester, 1774

When Dr. Johnson and Mr. and Mrs. Thrale stayed at Chester,
they visited the Cathedral, which, the scholar and moralist
remarked in his diary, was not of the first rank.

A disappointment, perhaps, while commenting that his father
had once visited the city's fair whilst he, when a child,
 suffered from smallpox.

Perhaps the red sandstone lacked rightful grace for a holy
 place—
too provincial, too monastic, too rooted in the earth, still
 tainted by plague spots.
Hewn roughly from the local quarries.

Or because of the absence of a vaulting spire pointing to
 heaven at which to marvel.
Still, the cloister, he conceded, was very solemn.

Dr. Johnson was, at least, delighted the Dean was pleased to
 see him.
Hester Thrale, it must be said, was even more direct
when she put her own words on paper.

Less concerned with giving due attention, moving in a hasty
 manner, dealing with the famous doctor's complaints, her
 husband's taciturn nature, and her daughter's apathy,
 she thought the Cathedral the poorest she had seen,
 the singing indifferent,

the altar giving everything a poverty of look, even if she in
 turn conceded
that she inhaled some venerable air in the mean edifice,
and felt the cloisters had a dignity of aspect.

They thought the medieval walls were wonderful, albeit
 useless and neglected.
They paced them commodiously, nonetheless, measuring
 precisely how far:
one mile, three quarters, and one hundred and one yards.

Noted, too, the periodic towers along the way, a Roman
 hypocaust in passing,
a stout, firm, subterranean arch in one street, and agreed:
 the city had many curiosities.

I wonder if they considered how the masons had soothed
 the moods of the sandstone. How they spoke to it, cajoling
 each block.
How well they knew it sheared with the grain.

How they prevented it from crumbling if cut against
 the bedding plane. How easy it was to dress.
How easy it was to fracture.

I wonder, before they went off to dine at Mold,
if they reflected on how through their work with chisel
 and mallet,
the masons were the keepers of a patient craft.

Herringbone Road

Laid close, wedged tight, set firm,
stone by stone in a herringbone weave,

against decay and forgetting,
resisting weather and time

remembering the hands that placed them,
then filled in the cracks with river sand

to limit the frost's bite,
the tilt and shift from the cart rattle,

to carry the earth's trade,
lead from hill, salt from inland mine to sea,

slate from quarry,
wool from valley farm,

bearing hoof and wheel, sacks and crates,
this fishbone, this backbone.

Salt Blooms Rising

Further on along the brine caverns,
into the shafts, stooping down,
the clogged air clamming skin,

gripping throats, voices crackling,
timbers groaning, hands blistering
from hauling, hoisting ropes,

cowd damp pressing,
bent to burden under the crust,
onward they go with dibbins and tubs

slopping, suffering the foisty tang,
slipping on glistening stone,
hoping the dripping roof will hold.

In the wych-house, the spittals
scraped and stirred, salt blooms rising,
gutter viewers following the brine

along the sheath, dipping gauges
red eyes stinging, blinking
with furred white lashes.

Crum dusts the floor, trodden along,
barmskins stiffen with residue.
Boilers crowding the lead pans,

feeding the flames, housseling,
their faces with sweat, broth
stirred into the simmering vat,

coaxing crystals from the edge
to corn within the water swirl,
pausing only to skeer the esse,

swinging hammer, blows
to the clinging salt cats
fingers raw, staggering,

stripped to the waist
dragging the rake, scraping
the scurf and bitter residue.

Children scurry in and out
with yelm-sticks, gathering
scrattings from corners and cracks.

White humps of sparkling salt,
sharp as frost caught in first light,
the flash pits spread, widening.

While the fields and streets subside.

Rushbearing

They go along the lanes,
ollerts, rantipoles, slummocks,
following the rushcart

dressed in ribbons, sodden garlands,
and crosses, creaking under the weight
of the new rushes cut before the sickness

from the river's edge and the wild marsh,
the hay from the meadows
before the first of the gleaning.

Heaped high for the flagstone floor,
sedge spread on cold ground, warm comfort
for the fretful and their faithful feet in winter.

Blessed across the threshold
with hymns, holy water, cow parsley,
a fiddler's tune and candle scent

to ward off the pestilence and fever,
the terrors of the night,
to keep away the rinderpest,

the wrath of the Lord, punishment
for the sins of the people, marked
by stones, drought and distress.

Splashing through the puddles,
jostling elbows to get in
through the inn doors,

mud caked above their ankles,
with pockets light, but hands quick,
eyes sharper still, faces flushed,

eager to wrestle and wager,
to celebrate the saint's day
with dancing, piety and affirmation.

The parson watches from the lychgate,
jaw set hard against the reek of ale,
the revelling slipping past reverence.

Cat Grin

There it is, over there.
If you look hard enough
you can see it, in the adder's grass.
That grin. Wide, knowing.
Teeth bared.

There it is, mischief bristling,
with gravel sticking to its tongue.
The whiskered trickster
is battle-stained, ghost-pawed.
Tail worn.

There it goes, padding along
the rutted road, following its own shadow,
wearing the wild like a second skin,
pouncing, claws piercing.
Fur scattering.

There it lingers, eyes glinting
beneath the lion's form,
below the snarling sandstone,
disappearing, reappearing.
A flawed brush stroke.

Crow Nets

A crow knows best
when the fields turn gold,

the ripened grain calling
louder than sermons.

Rooks chattering over barns,
thatch dishevelled, roystering

in marvellous decay,
testing the air,

tumbling, describing
a ragged circle.

Households bound
by netted law,

the Royal decree,
once each year to corvid catch.

Destroy the breed,
destruction stitched

with shrape before Michael's Feast.
Protecting bread and ale

from ravenous lawlessness.
Snare and kill the parliament,

murder the murder,
still the caw.

Mute the chatter,
quash the conspiracy,

cut through the confusion,
the commotion,

muster enough unkindness
to deal with the mob.

Spend the night
in storytelling.

Must stitch their traps,
sharpen their chaff,

make the trench,
tighten the knot,

lay cunning threads,
pin back lines,

with offal bait
across furrow and earth

to catch the old crows,
those rooks, those choughs.

No mercy for beaks
that rend the seed.

Pay a penny, half for three,
taken, netted, or slain,

quill scratch, debts tallied
in feathers and heads.

Keep the ordinance,
beware the neglect of duty.

When the crow nets lie idle,
feathers are untroubled by twine,

blunt splayed, swishing,
sweeping freely.

The kernelling corn
is easily plucked.

The black winged tide,
eyes watchful,

with dry-throat cry,
mocks across from the granary

as the mist lifts
from barley ricks.

Sunrise dimmed and darkened
by the murmuration of shadow,

crow-call, laughter, misrule,
across the straw and stubble.

Along the North and West Line

A familiar figure,
unassuming in manner,
highly esteemed,
always a staunch Conservative.

He shouldered the sample case,
brass-locked, road-scuffed,
filled with leather pattern books
of new lines, bolts of grey,

indigo-dipped prints,
picked up the podgy diary
crammed with itineraries,
maps with regular routes marked.

Names and addresses pencilled neatly,
order pads, train timetables,
a careful ledger of daily expenses,
obligation and a firm schedule.

Headed out on the road travelling
with the confidence of persuasion,
a manner rehearsed, smoothed out,
knowledge of profit margins,

a temperance pledge card,
moral rectitude, ready as ever
to extend credit, collect debts,
to note rival activity.

Calling before the station
on a family tailor emporium
behind the cathedral,
haggling over Lancashire grey,

visiting the high-end outfitters in the Rows,
then setting off on the North and West Line
choosing the coach with the better sprung seats
avoiding children, overtipping for luggage space,

to the drapers along the Marches,
noting the scenery, gathering anecdotes and recipes,
walking the length of burden along turnpikes,
bearing the heft of what will not be left behind.

Larks

Faith is a lamp burning steady.
The pilgrims pressed on.
The blood of the chosen
trickled into their voices,

and so, they rode out along the valley
through the forest,
up the steep hills in breaking storms,
steadfast,

carrying hand copied manuscripts
and pitch pipes,
gathering in the open,
in the places of soot and wool mills,

devotional labour,
poverty and upheaval.
Their routes took them across the moors,
tempests splitting the sky,

along sheep paths, stone tracks,
around scattered farms,
on to the bleak cloughside dwellings
inhabited by handloom weavers,

climbing up on muted ridges
with dissenting preachers,
marking bold stave lines,
saddle-worn singers and fiddlers,

with serpents and psalters in hand,
lifting their throats above the gales.
Psalms tucked under arms
singing and playing from the ground,

tilling furrows with prayer and song,
visions of a brighter shore,
with their backs to the wind
and grim, creeping death.

Rousing spirits in the hills,
cries of mercy resounding along
the upper Pennine fringes,
reaching deep to the heather roots,

balancing on the rim
of the green cup,
sliding down from Scout Moor
and Cribden Hill

to bring a lively graveyard tune.
The Layrocks infused the valley
with a vernacular
in fuguing style.

Marrowbone

Picked clean to ghost white,
kept in a battered tin pail,
rinsed beneath the well pump

cracked with a smack from the back of the cleaver,
a whispered prayer and a quiet utterance of thanks.

Boiled down slowly, it renders to broth,
swirling and sealing, thickening,
blessed, spooned out, shared

jellied and spread on coarse bread,
along with the salted dripping,

the residue of what lived strong,
what once moved with a slow purpose,
keeping the muscle in the limbs

knuckles and shinbones fished out
to hang over the pantry door,

clicking like grave-marked wind chimes
keeping the warmth, the hunger at bay,
the death from the chill weather away

some wrapped in cloth tied with a knot,
for luck, for remembering the bloodline

pumping along just under the skin,
oiling the gristle in the joints,
seen in the awkward twist of the hip

scratched into the fibres of the lungs,
flowing into the pulp of the rotting teeth,

to keep the splintering from the hearthstone,
the ache from the knees, the pain from the arching back,
some buried with care near the gooseberry bush roots

some burned to ash for the topsoil spread on the beetroot beds,
for growth and return, to renew the fire and steady the breath.

Longhope

There were not too many stories he felt he needed to relate
about his childhood, but towards the end,
before everything happened so suddenly,
he told me all he remembered about Longhope.

About going with his mother to visit family.
He could not recall who it was they stayed with
– an aunt perhaps – but he had a vivid memory
of a smallholding with two goats in a field.

And an orchard.

"How did you get there?" I asked.

"By train," he replied.

"I suppose the village had a station back then."

"It must have had."

"Tell me what else you remember," I continued.

"Other than the goats and the orchard, not much. I was
  about seven.
But I do remember the goats were standing by a gate and I
  stroked them."

"I wonder what kind of orchard it was," I said. "Cider
  apple, plum, perry pear?"

He looked as if he were pondering, wondering about this
   too.
Was there another memory coming back, a vague
   recollection?
Figures ladling dusk-red jam into jars?

We left Gloucestershire, meandered across the Atlantic,
and talked about how much fun it would be to visit
   Nuttallburg.
Fly all the way over to West Virginia, see the creeks and
   tributaries
where they found the coal, opened the mines, and wander
   around.

I smiled, thinking about this, remembering him,
when we went through Longhope, as we drove along the
   road
with its dips and bends, and the tall hedgerows,

passing through the narrow main street
with its small shop and post office, going on past All Saints,
taking in the landscape surrounding May Hill,

imagining the life of charcoal burners, coal miners, quarry
   workers,
the fruit pickers and jam makers, on our way to the forest
   and the trail
that leads to the view of the Wye from Symonds Yat.

Shore Pebbles

Wave-worn. Salt-scarred.
Wrack-tangled. Tide-wracked.

Scowdered by the sea wind,
shingle heaved from the underpull.

Stanes scattered along the spit.
Lain down slack, clitter-clatter,

afterdrag tugged, pebble-pale,
moon grey, grit luck sea snail.

A shoal of shore words
stitching the tideline to the bay.

Shale-splintered, tatties and chuckies,
discoids and piriforms rattling in the shallows,

skitters and flints, dulse-slicked, smoothed,
swaying bladderwrack, shilpit shimmering.

Hemming the tidemark, glasselled,
skin-scratched, sun-bleached on the skear,

on the scar flat, all limpet scabbed,
bruckle shells gathering along the wrackline.

Shilcock, hag-stoned,
salt-cured, surf-scrappers,

rock gullets in the smeeth stretch,
glaur-glistening, clinging,

wet palm clagginess, schist slipping,
silt sliding through fingers,

pocking pockets, shift and stutter,
kelp phlegm sticking to the lugworm castings.

Bright-eyed, cold-kissed peedie shells,
warmth-leached sand, hard-cast,

drift gathered, lap-lapping,
brine-lipped, dull clack clacking.

Gulls pause in the hush-lift,
fox-red in thick rainlight,

shillet flash, luck-white fish blink,
horizon wobble, seabed wreck shift.

Dreich drizzle, haar-rolled
crab-curling back. Scattering stanes.

Clatter-clitter, slack lain,
pale pibble, black cobble.

Sea-polished from storm surge,
turtle shell septarian nodules.

Spit-scattered, stutter tide,
dull clack, white rinsed.

Worn salted. Tangled wrack.
Shingle rigged, palm pebbly.

Storm stammer, starfish arm curl.
Scuttered skirl, tide twitch.

Land Stones

Another day's work. Bending, gripping,
pulling the land stones from the sodden field,
shaken loose from the furrows and ditches
by the plough and the spade, in the digging and the draining.

Scored hard in the long ache, the straightening effort,
the burden felt in the stretch and snap of the sinews
endured by the measure of a gnarling hunger.
Split, scattered, packed, scarred, cast away.

Pushed down, buried, when the old ice receded.
Found in the great heaps, preferred to the stones from
   the brook.
Some are pebbles, light and white as sun bleached
   knucklebone.
They can be held in the palm, turned, cast away like a
   half-formed thought.

Some are boulders and great slabs, too heavy to lift alone,
weighted down like the overbearing silence before a storm.
Others are decomposed granite and grit marble.
A lucky strike, making for good addlings.

The land does not stop birthing them.
They grow in the soil, the old ones say, are nudged, stirred,
encouraged by the seasonal inhalation and breath forced out,
teased to the surface by the rain and the frost,

loaded into carts and hauled away, crushed
to be set in roads and walls, or the granites
sent to the mason who shapes them
and chisels the names of the dead into.

Drift

Undertow

There is a sharp pull
beneath the waves.

Feel it, can you resist it,
gripping your ankles,

curling around, tightening
like a lover's enticing grasp,

clamping your cramping legs
tugging, dragging you

with the backwash
against the flow, away

from all you know,
with the undertow,

the sly taker under, calling
with such gentle persuasion

to the weary and the reckless,
those who stay too long

in the water, enchanted,
seduced, drifting further out,

flirting with the horizon,
losing touch with the shore,

forgetting the feel
of solid ground,

succumbing slowly,
abandoning resistance,

until limbs go numb
and breath turns shallow,

ignoring the darkening sky
and the undulation

daring to be drawn further
by the rip current in the sandbar,

pulled by the ebbing tide
past the line of breaking waves

towards the plunge point,
over to the break point,

into the deep, going under,
down to the bodies

and the wreckage
lying in the murk

where the light
does not reach.

Fen Lanterns

They glide and shimmy
with their warm inviting glow

through the reeds,
hovering over the marsh,

drifting beyond the sedges,
dancing in the mist

when the night is vast,
tricking the wanderers,

luring the unwary
into the boggy ground.

Those lucky enough
soon understand the deception

of the bobbing light,
the burning coal, the flicker flame,

when they hear the laughter,
barely making it back,

trying to find their way,
groping towards the homeward track,

stumbling, shaken, soaked through,
chilled to the bone,

bringing warnings to the lovers,
the heartbroken, bespoken,

the headstrong, the curious, the foolish,
churlish and confused,

treasure seekers, the bemused,
the desperate and lost,

the sorrowful, the whistlers,
melancholic, tormented,

night grifters and sinners—
to be aware of the jealous ones,

the oath-breakers, the unrighteous,
the wrongdoers, the pitiful cursed,

the forlorn, the tragic and misguided,
the wronged—

to beware of the wayward lanterns,
corpse candles,

and the stolen embers
that beckon and bewail.

But still they go.

Slipping Slack

Will you let this slide
away from the tether,
weightless, dissolving,
where nothing holds still,

into the flickering
the ripples unspooling
through the ribs,
lifting, turning, folding,

as the night creases,
the stars slipping slack
from their bearings
into the widening sea,

and not knowing if the tide
is carrying you home
or pulling you further
from the shore.

Into the Long Remembering

I lean on the wall
of the bridge for a while

before setting off
to walk along the tow path
to see you.

The river running below
is frothing white,
urgent, turbid,
tumbling over the weir
and the rocks.

The town is keeping
its weather chilled and wet.

From my distance,
the world along
the shadowed rift valley,

near the church in the woods,
into the hills
and the higher ridges,

seems older,
more brittle on the *allt*—
but my memory is hazy.

Heading up the track,
I pass through the open gate.

The crow castle ruin
comes into view,

the clouds slicing across its walls
like narrow scars.

The seam between earth and sky
is unravelling
through the glowering.

There is a heavy silence
between one shoulder
and the next.

I walk through dappled light
and quavering shade
as the path stretches and curves,

thinking that afterwards
I should head to the falls,
or the abbey ruins.

Yet it seems the sky
is thinking about darkening.
I sense a restlessness.

You do not notice me arrive.
You do not stir when I leave.

The room is crowded
with those you keep close,

their soft voices
calling you gently,
pulling you with them

before the final hush
into the long remembering.

Mud Crawler

My surroundings are rush-choked,
I feel as if I am crawling in mud,
sinking softly and without struggle.

Becoming something hidden
in the slick patches
of the soured silence

in the ooze and seep
where nothing settles
between solid ground and water.

Unremarked

I have started
to write short lists
of the overlooked things

I stop, more often now,
to notice when I walk
around the back fields,
along riverbanks,
the land's edges.

Perhaps to fill
a small notebook,
with a dark blue cover.

It has been lying on my desk
for a while,
looking for a purpose.

I just jot down
a few lines on a page.
Now and then.

Scribble in the margins.
Flick the pages back and forth.
Annotate. Delete.

—

ditch weed
with a bitter reek

ditchwater scummed
with something rotting

green bale twine
moss in the roofline of a shed

rain-slick sedge
grazers of decay

thistle and dock
a rusty hinge hanging loose
on an old barn doorframe

broad stone flags
on a disused threshing floor

nettles high around bins
up against a wall

a ten pence coin
muddied in a rain channel

a sheep itch scratch rubbing post
darkened by lanolin

a roofless kiln
with brick lime residue
and scuffed sign referring
to its heritage value

fresh fox prints
(NB: try to look harder
for fresh scat)

bruised windfall rotting sweet
wasp pickers

plough scar under barley
woodlice in the hollow
of a storm-felled tree trunk

ash dieback black on branches
a scruffy ewe watching from a brow
(although, all ewes seem scruffy)

shards of duck eggshell
(creamy, with brown specks…mallard?)

a half-ploughed strip
an oil sheen rainbow
in a puddle at the side of the road

slime scrolling
slug trails

blackthorn suckers
pushing through a gap in a wall

blue tarpaulin flapping
in the ruts of a tractor track

a cinder path
made from what was left

—

The lists keep getting longer.
I may even sort them
into categories.

I am avoiding, so far,
adding lists of the fly-tipped stuff—

the tyres, washing machines,
fridges, mattresses.

I would need more notebooks,
anyway.

Ferry

There were no hands to steady me.
No pull on my duffle coat hood.
No hold, no anxious screech to call me back.
No one to ask if I meant to let go.

That memory came to me suddenly,
and I was back there on the ferry,
braced against the rail, holding tight
against the wind, wondering where you had gone.

Watching the brown swill fold and furl,
listening to the waves slap against the bow,
concentrating on keeping my blurring vision focused,
ignoring and denying my worsening myopia.

Looking across to the other side, squinting,
barely making out the stacks and cranes,
the spires and blocks, The Three Graces,
along the blunt edged skyline. It wasn't all that far away.

And wondering about all that was below,
further down from the keel shadow's reach,
halfway across between Woodside and Pier Head,
beneath the crush of current and shifting silt.

Within the Great Hill

What was it that cut so deep?
How long did it take to be missed?
I suspect your words were softened by distance,

gradually, until they lost their weight
and you thought it would make it
all so much easier to carry.

There, within the great hill,
towering over the north parade
under persistent low clouds,

memories were captured, boxed,
stacked and stored,
though no-one knows where they went.

You did remember well, though,
the condensation forming,
ice thickening on the windows,

the eaves beading with rain,
damp patches on the ceilings,
grand rooms full of voices,

occasional laughter,
the receiving, unpacking lives,
being numbered, the deceiving tenderness,

the withheld truth,
fetching coal before breakfast
in the winter mornings,

the vegetable garden
behind the high stone wall,
the rotting apples,

the lifeboat heading
in the direction of Red Rocks
in a squall.

During the cold nights,
you stood on deck.
Cloaked in wool and fur,

focusing through brass spyglass,
searching for empty spaces,
beyond the bounds of charts,

spying a chipped blackened tooth
rising from a dark coast
scattered with volcanic peaks,

snow and hanging glaciers,
feeling a tangle
of excitement and dread.

On occasion, you wanted to believe
there was a kindness of sorts,
folded into starched linen,

with the stale crusts
given like treats,
and on day trips to the very edge

from where you would set out,
avoiding the muddy channel,
to Hildeburgh's island

drifting in tidal prayer,
doubted by those who waited
for miracles rising from parting sands,

listening to the wind
combing through the bracken
and slender grass,

the rattling lungs,
counting beads,
their faith yielding to the current,

bony fingers slipping
from the tenuous grasp
of sanctity.

The sea stretched endlessly,
at least it seemed to you,
out beyond the swash,

on Sunday walks
along the promenade.
It appeared to be as wide

as the hope to which you clung,
when you were fearful of letting go,
falling in, dragged around the point

and getting caught
in the slack tide.
You spoke of spectral figures

appearing unexpectedly,
shadows, inexplicable glimpses
dispersing just as quickly,

without reason.
Disappearances returning,
haunting those who remained behind,

holding on tight,
refusing to vanish
and be misplaced in the unquiet.

Myrtle Corner

Bog myrtle does not grow here now,
at least as far as I know.
And it was a long time ago

since the headland was covered with birch.
Only the names that are found on old maps,
and those I barely recall,

how they sounded in my mother's voice,
hint at what was,
in the pastures of lost ways.

A marsh farm of ghosts,
the dwelling on the rock,
clenched against the tide

down by the hazel spring,
the saint's half-forgotten church of oak,
the slipways and field edges.

The goat-fold track winding
from the great stone ridge
and its rain-polished flints,

down to where the sallows grow
along the boundary of the assembly field,
seaward through unplotted ground.

The dark fortress, the cold hill,
the Island of the Welsh,
the village of the Irish,

the Frenchman's farm,
Bruna's riverbank, the hollows,
the shieling, the trench, klakkr tun.

The windswept shoreline,
fog bound reefs,
the stronghold by the grove, the nook,

the sluggish stream, the swift river,
the fenders and ditches,
the ford for sea rovers,

the valley by the sea, the thorn tree,
the island where the prizefighters
at dawn raised fists heavy with secrecy,

and the phantom fires flickered
amid the chaos.
This corner is between two estuaries,

neither one nor the other,
never on the fringes,
shaped by departures,

crossings over the mudflats,
and words shifting,
stretching in the throats

of those who left cwm and ffridd
for low fields and this liminal ground,
who gripped their names tightly,

and never forgot
to turn their gaze,
occasionally, westwards.

The Streets

I walk along, unsure,
feeling exposed, obvious,
anxious, ignoring the stares,
the attitude, trying to avoid

the concrete and bricks,
the dogs and their sticks,
the man with the mumble,
trying to remember my survival Scouse,

hoping I will not trip
and stumble. Going on past
the Welsh chapels, thinking
of those who came from the west

to the wild east from the slate lands,
the coal fields, from the fishing places,
and the brickyards, to build the harbour,
the skyline, pave the streets,

passing the windows now shuttered
with metal sheets. It all breathes, still,
through the gaps of the crumbling walls,
graffiti daubing the tinned-up houses,

hanging in the glares, along the terraces
where demolition looms/renovation begins.
There are those who see something desirable
in the condemned, who love the sturdy character

despite the vacant surroundings,
who feel history seems nicer
when you scrub out the past.
There are few who were reluctant holdouts,

few who looked with fondness
on the rising damp, the fungus,
the slow rot — few who could resist
the managed decline and miraculous revival.

I find the site where my great-grandfather's family
had their butcher shop.
There is nothing there now.
I did not expect anything else.

Delicate Fracturing

The morning
is caught
in a moment
of dim light

and stillness,
between
gleam
and rising.

Hoarfrost thickens
on the trees—
spun-silk traces,
subtle and intricate,

interlace and loop
through the limbs,
embroider branches,
catch the sun's glitter.

Lines marble along
the rough grain of fence posts.
Rhew insinuates itself
into the seams

glaar slicks
over the gate hinges,
hard above,
soft beneath.

Low mist creeps up
from the river meadows,
hangs in the fold,
drifts over the pasture.

A blackbird drops
from the orchard hedge,
scatters skrim
from the grass tips.

Feeds low,
tail flicks.
Lifts
with muted wings.

Rime clings
to each step.
The silence is split
by the sound

of ground
cracking,
boots crunching
puddle crizzle.

Everywhere,
a delicate fracture.
I listen. For how things are
after breaking.

The General Synopsis at 0600

Low Fair Isle, 981,
new lows expected Viking 986
and North Utsire 990,

drifting slowly east,
cyclonic gathering,
air thickening,
threat of hard bickering.

The area forecasts for the next 24 hours:

Viking, North Utsire, South Utsire

West winds scouring
pointed skerries,

flukra dusting tips of rocky isles
pulled further offshore,

cauldron tossed waves,
sjøsprøyt rising wild,

sild in mustard, marinading,
dialect hauled from the depths in nets,

rye tongue tangled,
words growling,
growing fierce.

Forties, Cromarty, Forth

Wild hooley blowing raw,

thick set haar solidifying further,
churning seas roughening, skirling,

cliffs spray blurred,
deepening dreich gloom,

fleeting, lost, yillen,
altocumulus stippling
into mackerel sky, scaling,
storm imminent.

Tyne, Dogger, Fisher, German Bight, Humber

Winds veering cyclonic,
graupel tickling, tide rising,

eel-slick mudflat oozing,
Deichgraf warnings sharpening,

voices mingling in sands,
riddles, sea-clay phrasings,

spindrifting, bitterly klar,
dull later.

Thames, Dover, Wight, Portland, Plymouth

Southwest gusts whitening cliffs,

mizzle drifting inland,
fields sodden,
chalk whispering,
shingle scratching,

histories rasping,
arrivals landing on flint pebbles,

daily, roughening, persistent.

Biscay, Trafalgar, FitzRoy

Northeast winds gathering slowly,

orbela, brétema, marusia choppy,
sprats scattering,

glass falling, decks slickening,

low tide sea smell,
lively marejada,

horizon slipping,
kinetosis swell,

cloudburst, reluctant at first,
feeling stubborn.

Sole, Lundy, Fastnet, Irish Sea, Shannon

Southerly winds,
waves emerald,

droimníní breaking softly,
ceobhrán valley veiling,

rain falling,
brine-bitten gossip piercing,

throats raw,
white horses galloping,

pressure dropping,
tending towards severe.

Rockall, Malin, Hebrides

West gales roaring, waves phenomenal,

kelp flinging wide,
kelpies submerging,

selkie skins scattering,
remaining human for a while,

machair flattening,
peat smoke curling,

cloud heavy tumbling,
isobars stretched taut,
ice in the rigging.

Bailey, Fair Isle, Faeroes, South-east Iceland

Northern winds harsh,
cod banking, fearn kist, unpredictable,

kishies swinging,
owsins sloshing,

accumulating, kavi,
ice forming,

drángar stark ahead
and frost-etched,

snjór blanketing
mountain shoulders,
isköld sjór swallowing.

Denmark Strait

The pious words
of the wind and sea ritual
drift out across the black stillness.

The salt-etched names
float and roll in the steady swell,
cutting through the fog bank.

The voice of the storm
sways in measured chants.
Less a recitation,
less a rote declaration.
More an incantation.

It brings the distant weather,
the poor visibility,
the imminent gales gathering breath,

the swirling currents,
the sharpening gusts,
sleet-lashed decks,

the spatter at dawn,
close to shore in fleeting syllables
over the barnacle encrusted airwaves

for all those who are moored safely
or landbound in the quiet
before sleep.

I missed it
when there was no longer mention
of Denmark Strait.

It slipped away,
veered without warning,
like a moderate surge,

far beyond the familiar crackle,
dimming the occasional brightness,
dissolving gently into the persistent drizzle,

fading with the intermittent,
becoming distant
when the boundaries of the sea areas
were adjusted.

But that did not make the forecast
any quieter,
the outlook less unsettled,

burn away the patches of mist
or bring cautious hopes
for a calmer outlook.

Nor did it reduce the static,
the subsonic roar,
or the slowly rising pressure.

It just washed in a feeling
of losing something
I could never hope to grasp.

Until I crossed it
in an August gale.

It is a comfort to know
it is there
and feels as wild and remote

as I imagined the high seas to be
in the night,

all those years ago,
tuning in, wishing, dreaming.

And then, there I was.
Making my way
from the hard, jagged edges
of Blosseville Coast
to the shelter of Ísafjörður.

Far Ridge

I

The ridge turns sharply along its shoulder,
the distance folds into the curve.

The contours draw the eye
without teasing a promise of arrival.

I begin to feel the weight of staying still,
rooted, sensing the leaving before I choose it.

I watch the slow retreat of the cloud shadow
from the upper tract. There's no path, no marker,

just the thinnest ripple lifting and revealing
the bare suggestion of a way forward.

Noticing a thin hawthorn with cracked bark
near a collapsed section of drystone wall,

I make my way over, thinking it a perfect place to sit.
For a while, at least, on what remains of the shaded side.

The wall leans precariously further along at the midsection,
doing just as well to keep things in and out.

II

I have walked here so many times,
getting to know this wind-scrubbed
ground rising and leaning
away from the sky.

I sat, listened and looked across,
reckoning with how much
of what was here, what appeared fixed
had already drifted from view.

It was quite the temptation to stay longer
in the comfort of what was providing shelter,
to enjoy the breeze and the silence,
but I made the effort

to stand, shoulder my pack
and get moving again,
feeling a slight sluggishness in my legs,
the kind that soon loosens.

There is more ground to cover,
there are more gates to open,
close behind me, more paths to take
that stretch to the long reach.

There is more on the map to read and follow,
there are more routes to plan and plot,
more bearings to take with my compass,
there is more terrain to navigate across.

I can see stone walls ahead to rest against
every now and then, just close enough
in the distance to make me want to reach them
and see what lies beyond the far ridge.

Track Reappearing

Some tracks do not remain visible,
as you make your way.

Like the hard splintered white road
pulling outward along the ancient seabed,

the chalk ridge with its flinty grit,
its sticky weight of red-brown clay.

There are times when it is clear,
when it bends towards a rise

where a sarsen boulder rests,
leaning eastward over from a cross-ridge dyke.

There are times when it closes in on itself,
becomes a cambered stretch running on the crest,

recent rainwater draining along either side,
leading in the direction of a long barrow.

There are times when it fades from sight,
yet can be felt underfoot in the cut and fill.

I remind myself to be patient.
It reappears in the right catch of light,

just as when it came back into view,
when I wandered off course,

losing the earth rise, focused on potsherds
exposed in the plough soil scatter

going past the boundary stone,
shoulder height, lichen patched

in short grass on the oval bank
down by the thickened rib

and the deep grim trench
near the bachelor's hill

into a shallow dip
on the outer lip

where the gorse was close grown,
when every trace of it had been lost on the map.

Turnaround Point

There is always a place like this,
an eventual point reached.

Celebrated by neither sign nor view.
No visible landmark, at least.

No indication.
No intimation.

One recognised through
an unspoken agreement
between body and land.

Knowing it is there
through the give of the ground.

The way continues winding
towards a narrowing,
leading to a sheltering fold.

You feel you could go on,
following it as far as it will take you.

You pause.
Not because you are tired.

You realise you have come
much further than you thought,
even though you had set off slowly,

without counting the steps,
without wondering how long it would take.
To reach here.

Enough time has passed
to forget where you started.

Perhaps it is because of how
the clouds drift low,
the way the wind drops,

and the feeling
of that recurrent shiver
creeping down your spine,

that you want to stop, turn back,
and revisit all that you missed along the way.

Coda

These poems began in fragments and memories. Small, fleeting, but never forgotten. A dialect word, a trick of light, a family story replete with themes of pilgrimage, ancient battles and standing stones, the sensation of ground giving way underfoot, trying to glimpse what lingers beyond the line of sight. A coastal cliff-edge moment – a metaphorical one – of confrontation with danger, connections to people and place, and all there is to look forward to. A musing on the weathering of rock and human ageing; the slow processes of erosion, the faster reshaping of the mind and body, and acceptance. A moment in a walk – or one's point in life – where instinct prompts the thought of turning back, shaped by mood and place. Coastal attentiveness and pondering a small drama of intertidal goings on. Although not so small seen from the perspective of the creatures involved in them. Heading along ancient tracks and ridgeways.

And then there is a reflection on stories of what was experienced in Brynmor, a children's home where my mother spent some years living – the name originating from the Welsh bryn mawr, meaning great hill (or big or high hill, depending on variants). On the coast at the point where the River Dee flows out into the Irish Sea, at the old high lake that once provided a safe anchorage, it was a long way from the old family life and treasured stories of Llanfairfechan – the little church of St. Mary. Yet the stories told from that time within the great hill were some of the earliest I heard.

One recurring theme is extraction, and the marks it leaves. On Mynydd Helygain/Halkyn Mountain in Sir y Fflint/Flintshire, the traces of lead mining remain visible beneath the thin skin of heather and grass, but to walk there is to encounter ecological resilience. Near Wrecsam/Wrexham, the spoil heap from Bersham colliery remains unsettled, sparking controversy over whether it is heritage, eyesore, or both at once. Slate quarries have cut deep into the hillsides of Gogledd Cymru/North Wales, and stories of danger, class division, defiance, and labour unrest have been passed down.

I am fascinated with how to go about working down and into the strata of language and dialect, how it runs through the deep time of place and landscape, how it brings out the texture of daily life. I have always been drawn to old Cheshire words and phrases that hold soil, weather, and toil within them. For example, fox bench is an impermeable subsoil layer in the sandstone underlands of Cheshire and Flintshire, impeding agriculture and field drainage. As stubborn and sly as its name suggests. Backen means "to delay, to keep back." In 1877, Egerton Leigh published *A Glossary of Words Used in the Dialect of Cheshire* and gives an example of its use: "This fou weather backens ploughing." I wove this into the poem, which imagines being accompanied by the spectral presence of folk from not that long ago who worked the land and who spoke a rural vernacular anchored in everyday work, place, and the earth. Nizzly means "inclined to rain, foggy, drizzly" (again, thanks to Leigh for this concise definition – I remember what it means well, but this is precise too). These lines should be self-explanatory – the practice of using rock salt as hygrometer to forecast the weather, with its dreeping (dripping) on the floor where twitch clogs (black beetles) scutter. Ackersprit is a word describing potatoes when the roots have germinated before the time of harvesting them. The poem reflects on drought and poor harvests in 19th century Cheshire. Today, in the era of climate change, we would likely consider ackersprit to be a vital indicator word of environmental rupture. We need to hang on to such words.

Language as memory is a theme running through these poems, but so too is the idea of language as drift and how coastal glossaries can form and reshape with the ebb and flow: such as tide-worn words for pebbles, wrack, and shells. The Shipping Forecast, with its sea-area names spoken like incantations, carries its own rhythm, half liturgical, half meteorological. And so, there are a couple of poems that are a shoal of shore words and pull coastal dialect from the sea areas around the British Isles and the northern North Atlantic, dropping them into the waves and swell to be tossed around by the stormy weather.

Another undercurrent is family, and the fragments of inheritance that linger in gesture, habit, body, work, or story. The days of a commercial traveller in North Wales, Cheshire, and further south along the Welsh Marches (inspired by imagining what my great-grandfather's journeys would have been like); my father's childhood recollection of goats and an orchard in Longhope, a village in Gloucestershire from where his mother's family originated; the bones that were either boiled down in kitchen pots until marrow turned to strong broth, or which were hung over pantry doors as ritual acts. Or burnt to ash for scattering on the soil.

Fleeting moments matter because they cannot always be grasped, and perhaps never possessed even if they can be caught. They are gone as soon as they arrive, leaving behind the sense that something has shimmered, glimmered and can only catch the eye, however briefly, before slipping away.

Land, language, and memory endure, though. Spoil heaps become places of argument about community and the erasure of history; walls moss over yet retain the initials someone carved into them long ago. Landscapes are also threaded with uncanny presences: ghostly watchers glimpsed in the

Berwyn mists; corpse candles swaying over fenland; that feline trickster the Cheshire Cat. These figures exist in thresholds, weather, and stories. Yet something always appears and remains that is spectral, furtive, fugitive, restless. Surfaces slip beneath, remerge, become something other.

www.ingramcontent.com/pod-product-compliance
Lightning Source LLC
LaVergne TN
LVHW010307070426
835512LV00029B/3500